Color My Mandalas

LOUISE ATHERTON

COLOR MY MANDALAS

2017 Louise Atherton

ISBN: 1544899998
ISBN-13: 978-1544899992

LOUISE ATHERTON

tranquility

COLOR MY MANDALAS

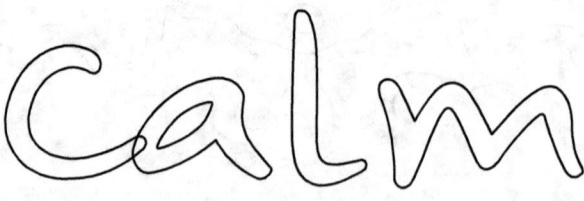

LOUISE ATHERTON

LOUISE ATHERTON

Softness

Dance

LOUISE ATHERTON

LOUISE ATHERTON

comfort

LOUISE ATHERTON

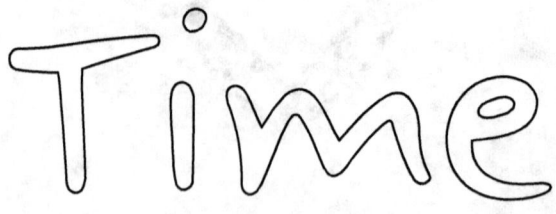

LOUISE ATHERTON

smell

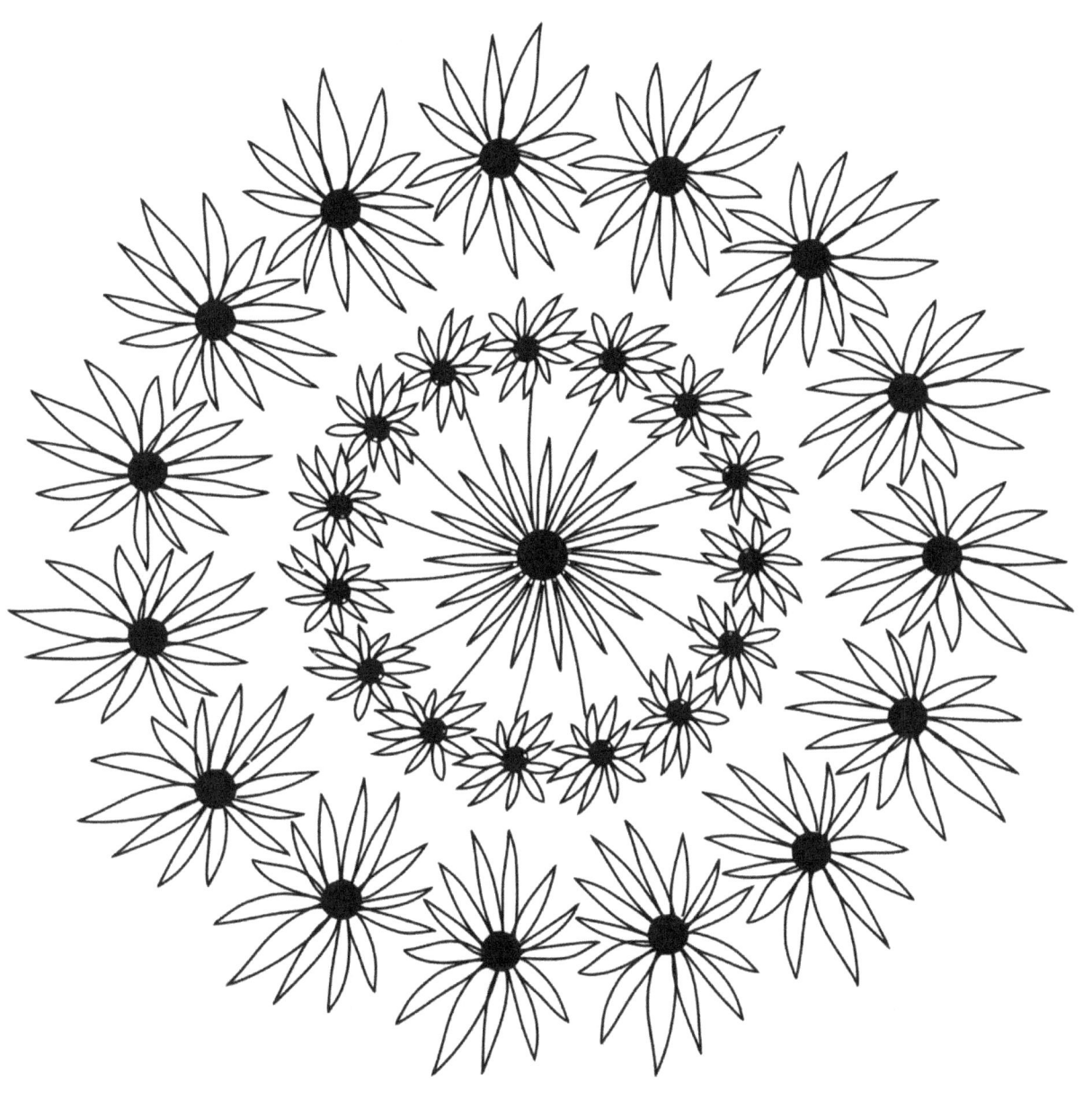

LOUISE ATHERTON

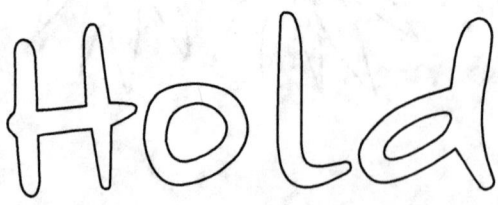

LOUISE ATHERTON

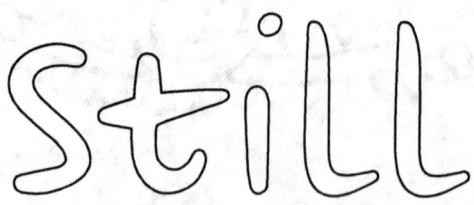

Serene

LOUISE ATHERTON

Senses

COLOR MY MANDALAS

LOUISE ATHERTON

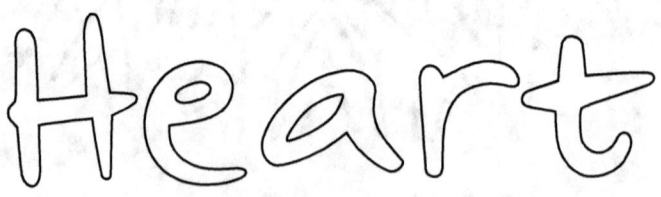

Joyous

LOUISE ATHERTON

Harmony

LOUISE ATHERTON

Belonging

Together

Release

LOUISE ATHERTON

COLOR MY MANDALAS

www.ingramcontent.com/pod-product-compliance
Lightning Source LLC
Chambersburg PA
CBHW081253180526
45170CB00007B/2410